essentia

Writing Great Copy

Time-saving books that teach specific skills to busy people, focusing on what really matters; the things that make a difference – the *essentials*. Other books in the series include:

Making Great Presentations

Speaking in Public

Responding to Stress

Succeeding at Interviews

Solving Problems

Hiring People

Getting Started on the Internet

Writing Good Reports

Feeling Good for No Good Reason

For full details please send for a free copy of the latest catalogue.
See back cover for address.

The things that really matter about

Writing Great Copy

Sallyann Sheridan

ESSENTIALS

For Christopher, my son, friend
and greatest teacher, with unending love.

Published in 1999 by
How To Books Ltd, 3 Newtec Place,
Magdalen Road, Oxford OX4 1RE, United Kingdom
Te: (01865) 793806   Fax: (01865) 248780
email: info@howtobooks.co.uk
www.howtobooks.co.uk

British Library Cataloguing in Publication Data.
A catalogue record for this book is available from
the British Library.

Edited by Diana Brueton
Cover design by Shireen Nathoo Design
Cover copy by Sallyann Sheridan
Produced for How To Books by Deer Park Productions
Typeset by Anneset, Weston-super-Mare, Somerset
Printed and bound in the United Kingdom

NOTE: The material contained in this book is set out in good faith for
general guidance and no liability can be accepted for loss or expense
incurred as a result of relying in particular circumstances on
statements made in the book. Laws and regulations are complex and
liable to change, and readers should check the current position with
the relevant authorities before making personal arrangements.

ESSENTIALS *is an imprint of*
How To Books

Contents

Preface

In an increasingly competitive world, the ability to write compelling words (copy) is a valuable skill to have.

You may have the best product or service in the world, but that's not enough. To stay in business *you need to sell those products and services.* Or maybe you want to sell your ideas to a potential backer, or yourself to a prospective employer. Either way, you'll be using words, and you'll stand a far *greater chance of success* if you *acquaint yourself with the essentials of copywriting.*

Whether you're writing letters, brochures, advertisements, packaging, press releases, commercials, applications or posters, you can improve them all when you start applying basic copywriting techniques. Whether you're a full time copywriter or someone who's called upon to write copy every now and then, keep this book close to hand. *Your writing, and your sales, will never be the same again.*

Sallyann Sheridan

1 Before You Write

Coming up with ideas is the easy bit.
Knowing how to sell them is what counts.

5 things that really matter

1 ASSESS YOUR COPYWRITING SKILLS

2 CHECK WHAT YOU'RE SELLING

3 DECIDE WHO YOU'RE SELLING TO

4 CONSIDER HOW YOU'RE GOING TO SELL

5 USE TRIED AND TESTED FORMULAS

Words are *everything* in marketing, whether they're written or spoken. You can **make an average letter great** simply by changing a few words. Or turn an unsuccessful advert into a successful one by rephrasing what's on offer. And by using the tried and tested formulas used by professional copywriters you can **consistently transform dull messages into words that sell**.

When writing copy, **planning isn't preferable or desirable, it's essential**. That's because copywriting isn't just a bland presentation of the facts

- It's about defining exactly *what* you're selling and who you're selling it to.
- It's knowing which words will arouse desire in the reader.
- It's understanding how to phrase offers and instructions in a way that will motivate and get the reader to act.
- And it's about reassuring them once they've decided to do so.

IS THIS YOU?

• *My boss has asked me to write a sales letter promoting our new stationery range. Where do I start?* • *Lots of young people come into our factory shop especially to look at our own brand cosmetics, but very few buy. Someone suggested I rewrite the packaging copy. Help!* • *My advert in the local press just isn't working. I can't understand why when everyone says there's such a shortage of reliable plumbers in the area.*

 ASSESS YOUR COPYWRITING SKILLS

Copywriting is a skill you can learn. In essence, it's about writing which **sells**, **promotes**, **informs**, **raises awareness**, or **instructs**. Business or marketing skills, if you already have them, may be useful, but they're not essential.

It helps if you:

● **Have a reasonable command of the language**, although you don't need great literary skills or perfect grammar.

● **Have an interest in words.** As a copywriter, words are your tools.

● **Enjoy finding out about new things**.

You can help yourself further by:

● **Becoming an avid reader** of other people's copy (read advertisements, sales letters, advertising posters, packaging, anything you can lay your hands on. See which messages work best on you).

● **Analysing all you read** (ask yourself why those words, headings and messages persuaded you to buy that new after shave, perfume, car or holiday).

- **Becoming someone who asks questions** (about everything and everyone. How else will you find out all you need to know about the product you're writing about or the person you're writing for?).

As with all skills, **practice and more practice** is the key. The beauty of using this book as your guide is that **you can learn in one hour what other copywriters have taken years to learn**. Take advantage. Use the tried and tested formulas, tips and techniques of professionals and you'll soon be writing winning copy.

You don't want people to read your copy and say, 'That's lovely writing.' You want them to say, 'I must have that product!'

CHECK WHAT YOU'RE SELLING

As a copywriter, you need to know exactly **what you are selling**. Find out all you can about the **product**, **person**, or **service** you're writing about. This will help your writing even though you probably won't include all you've learned.

Imagine you're writing an advertisement to sell a book. Do people buy books? No, they buy ways to entertain themselves, to learn and to improve their lives. If the book is about make-up tips, you're offering the reader an opportunity to:

- look better and healthier
- appear younger
- increase their self-esteem
- raise their confidence levels.

In turn, this might:

- improve their job prospects

- increase their financial security

- improve their relationships.

These are some of the **benefits** of the book which you need to convey to your prospect. Otherwise they'll glance at your material and think, 'So what?' That's why it's essential to examine your product or service carefully to **determine what the real benefits are**. Because that's what you're truly selling or offering.

To **avoid confusing the benefits of a product or service with its features**, consider the following. If the make-up book has a wipeable cover, that's a **feature** of the book. If it's fully illustrated throughout, that's also a feature. You may find it useful to list features as a way of helping you determine what the true benefits of your product or service are.

Everything has a **Unique Selling Proposition (USP)**. This is something about you, your product or service which is unique. Something which is different from your competitor. Maybe you're the *only* job applicant with relevant experience. Perhaps you're the *only* baby food manufacturer to include a sterile wrapped baby's spoon with the product. Although the spoon is a feature, you can turn it into a benefit in terms of health, convenience and saving time and money. Or maybe you're the *only* computer servicing company in your region which doesn't charge for call-outs. Capitalise on your **uniqueness** in your copy.

'What's in it for me?' is all anyone asks. And if your copy doesn't answer that question rapidly, it won't get a second glance.

DECIDE WHO YOU'RE SELLING TO

When you write copy you may be tempted to try to write in a way that will appeal to everyone. That's because you obviously want your words to attract the attention and response of as many people as possible. Whatever you're selling it's unlikely to have a universal appeal. Your product, service, ideas, or unique skills will usually appeal to **a particular group of people** and it's those people you should **target**.

The better you understand your reader, the greater chance you have of writing copy that will appeal to him or her. It often helps to **build a profile** of the sort of person you're trying to attract with your copy. Imagine you are selling a new brand of horse feed which, according to research, keeps horses healthier. You would target horse and stable owners, possibly vets. If your budget prohibits you from targeting all these categories separately, decide which one you're going to concentrate on. Which one will be the most lucrative?

If you decide to target horse owners, you need to have a typical owner in mind. Questions you might ask yourself are:

- Which newspapers and magazines do horse owners read?
- Which radio and TV stations do they listen to most?
- How old are they?
- Where do they live?
- What's their average income?
- On average, what's their annual vets' bill?

Whatever or whoever you're researching, **you need to arrive at a typical reader and write with them in mind**. The more specific you are, the better your copy will be, providing you've got your research right, of course. You can even imagine your typical reader's hair colour and style – anything which helps you.

If your product is a compact disc featuring a live concert of a heavy metal band, your average target reader may be completely different from the horse owner. Possibly younger, less affluent, and a reader of entirely different magazines. This illustrates how essential it is to **have a reader in mind before writing copy**. The language, incentives and tone would differ greatly in these examples.

You may have heard people talking about selling business to business. But all business is conducted between people, individually or collectively. You are always communicating with a person in that business and your copy must be written with that person in mind. Ask yourself questions before you write, such as:

- Does my product or service solve their particular problems?
- Will it be a cost-effective option for them?
- Will it improve their standing in the company?

Remember, whatever you write it will be read by a person, an individual, and that's who you're writing to. **There's no such thing as business to business advertising**.

Remember to write with a specific individual in mind.

 CONSIDER HOW YOU'RE GOING TO SELL

As a copywriter, you cannot write a word without knowing where those words are to appear. Consider the following:

- magazine advertisements (general, specialist, business and trade)

- newspaper advertisements (national, regional and local press)
- commercials for the television, radio or cinema
- internet/web page adverts
- advertorials (adverts in magazines and newspapers that look and read like editorial)
- press releases
- poster advertising (at underground stations, on buses, on billboards)
- sales letters
- point of sale displays
- company or product information brochures and catalogues.

The merits of each of these different forms of advertising need to be assessed according to your other research and budget. If you've decided that your typical customer is likely to be an 18-year-old male music lover you wouldn't place adverts in a retirement magazine. You may however consider placing them in the popular music press and dynamic posters on high profile sites.

Each marketing option also presents you with different challenges. You could write hundreds of words in a sales letter, for example, but far fewer on a poster or in a small ad. Other **things you need to establish** are:

- Do you want the reader to buy straight from the advertisement? If so you need to include availability and/or ordering details.
- Do you want to be contacted for further information? Put contact details.

- Will photos or images accompany your writing?
- What is the 'life' of your advert, will it appear in a daily newspaper or an annual directory?
- Will your words be read, or listened to as in a radio commercial?

If you're writing packaging copy, for a small carton, box or blister pack, for example, the amount of space you have to write in is restricted. So first you need to **establish what you're legally required to show on the packaging** – a list of contents perhaps, ingredients, symbols, cautions or warnings. Once you know this you can see exactly how much space you have left in which to sell the product. Don't be tempted to cram in too much copy otherwise the print size will be so small that people won't be able to read it. At times like this you need to produce **tightly written copy** and this is an excellent exercise to sharpen your skills.

Decide where your words will appear, who will see or hear them, and what you want them to do – make sales, generate enquiries or raise product awareness.

 USE TRIED AND TESTED FORMULAS

A great way to get started is to use formulas developed by successful marketing professionals. **AIDA**, an acronym for **Attention, Interest, Desire, Action**, is a tried and tested copywriting formula which professionals continue to use.

AIDA:

- First you get your reader's **attention**.
- Then you arouse their **interest** in your product or service.

- Now you lead them to **desire** your product or service.

- Finally, make the desire strong enough to get them to **act** (order, phone, or whatever you've asked them to do).

AIDA is useful in many sales situations including newspaper and magazine advertisements and sales letters.

- **Attention** can be caught by powerful headlines which communicate the main benefit of the product or service you're selling.

- **Interest** can be aroused by expanding on this benefit and outlining others which appeal to your reader's self-interest.

- **Desire** can be created by touching their emotions – show how others have become more attractive/wealthy/intelligent/healthy/secure/confident using this product. Use testimonials.

- **Action** can be prompted if you reassure the reader they're making the right decision and make it easy for them to do so. Make ordering easy and offer guarantees.

Another successful formula, particularly effective when writing sales letters and other direct marketing methods, is Bob Stone's Formula:

- Put your main benefit first.

- Expand upon the main benefit and introduce secondary benefits.

- Tell the reader exactly what they'll get (in full).

- Back up your copy with case histories, testimonials and endorsements.

- Tell your reader what they may 'lose' if they fail to act.

- Restate all the benefits you've mentioned – except this time phrase them in a different way.
- Incite the reader to act immediately.

No need to reinvent the wheel – begin by using formulas which have been tried and tested.

MAKING WHAT MATTERS WORK FOR YOU

✓ Assess your current level of copywriting skills and improve those areas you need to work on.

✓ Planning is essential. Establish where your words will appear and how much space that gives you.

✓ Understand what you're selling by identifying the true benefits of the product or service.

✓ Identify a typical reader or listener of your copy – and then write for them.

✓ Utilise the successful tried and tested formulas developed by professionals.

✓ Give yourself a deadline – and stick to it!

2 Words – A Copywriter's Tools

Make your message clear. The reader won't struggle to understand what you've written. Nor should they.

5 things that really matter

1 **CHOOSE WORDS THAT SELL**
2 **ENSURE READABILITY**
3 **MAKE IT PERSONAL**
4 **WRITE ATTENTION-GRABBING HEADLINES AND SUBHEADINGS**
5 **MAKE BODY COPY INTERESTING AND IMPORTANT**

The dictionary describes a copywriter as someone who writes advertising copy. Most people can write, but as any successful copywriter knows **there is an art to writing compelling copy**. And the art is in **the words you choose and the order in which you place them**. These decisions will make or break your advertising material. Get it right and sales can soar, get it wrong and sales can plummet. It's worth remembering too that whilst the words you write might not be great literature, they can have a profound effect on people's lives. A retired couple might take a trip of a lifetime because of something you've written, or a young woman may be inspired to study towards a more fulfilling career.

Of course, all writing is about selecting words, whether you're writing a letter, a magazine article or a novel. But with so much money literally riding on every word, copywriters are under pressure to get it right far more often than not.

IS THIS YOU?

● A year ago, I started a company which develops accounting software. We have a great product, but we can't seem to get the message across to people. ● I work as a freelance computer trainer and although I've sent letters out to training companies who say they've got lots of work, not one has contacted me. Any ideas? ● I spent a fortune on a full-page advert and so far my one-man business has two jobs from it – which hasn't even covered the cost of the advert. Where did I go wrong?

 CHOOSE WORDS THAT SELL

Words are your tools. You will use them to guide, persuade, inspire, reassure, motivate and create desire in the reader to reach a favourable conclusion about you, your product or service. You will use them to encourage people to respond, perhaps within a given time, and to make people feel good about that decision. And you will **touch your readers' emotions** – explain how you're going to make them happier, richer or safer. And if you want your reader to get enthusiastic about what you're selling, **your words have to convey your enthusiasm**.

Imagine you're selling a product which will offer your reader security and peace of mind. You wouldn't want to simply list its features and attributes and say, 'This will make you secure'. Consider instead words and phrases such as:

● Never again will you need to worry about . . .

● . . . gives you complete peace of mind.

● You will rest easy knowing . . .

● You'll never have to take chances again.

Always check every word to see whether there's a better one available. Don't just say *Made in Europe*, consider alternatives such as *hand tooled in* . . . or *created, developed* or *designed*. And, when space permits, mention the *attention to detail*, the fact that it's *custom built* and *exceeds the exacting standards required by* . . . It really is a case of **the more you tell, the more you sell** – provided you use the right words.

Use strong verbs – *astonish* your friends, *capture* the mood of, *dazzle* your colleagues, *discover* the secrets of, *indulge* yourself in, *relish* the delights of, *tantalise* your partner, *soothe* away aches, *unleash* the power of, *astonish* your family, *crush* pain, *deliver* instant relief, *explore* your sexuality, *celebrate*, *worship*, *frolic*, to name a few.

Consider the difference between *find* and *discover*. *Discover the secrets of* . . . sounds more interesting than *find the reasons behind* . . .

Clichés (well-worn phrases) are shunned in most writing, except copywriting. That's because **clichés work in advertising** and you'll discover them in most copy:

- Buy now, pay later.

- Limited number available.

- 100% satisfaction guaranteed.

- The seven deadly sins of . . .

- Fits like a glove.

Clichés are often a rapid way of getting your message across. Use them only after careful consideration and use them sparingly.

Remember, something is either new or improved – it can't be both.

 **ENSURE READABILITY**

As the writer, the onus is on you to write in a way your reader will understand. That's why it's essential to gauge as accurately as possible who will be reading your copy. But whoever you're writing for, most copy is read quickly, so it needs to be **easy to understand**. That doesn't mean talking down to your reader, it simply means **communicating clearly**.

- Use shorter words (car instead of vehicle).

- Make clear statements and claims (money back guarantee if not absolutely delighted).

- Avoid long sentences.

- Make the words, sentences and paragraphs flow easily into one another.

- Be specific (what does quality and style actually mean with regard to your product?).

- Avoid inappropriate humour (if in doubt, leave it out).

The other thing you need to avoid is jargon and overuse of acronyms. You may know that SAD stands for seasonal affective disorder and RSI stands for repetitive strain injury, but don't assume your reader will. It's always best to write out the phrase in full in the first instance and to put the acronym in brackets immediately after. You can then refer to it by its acronym thereafter. For instance: *Repetitive strain injury (RSI) is now a thing of the past for Nikki Giles. But when she was first diagnosed with RSI, she . . .*

Clarity is essential in all copy. Your reader isn't reading a book or magazine which they've chosen from a library, bookstore or news stand. They haven't got to read what you've written, so unless you make it easy, they won't bother. Ensure your message is easily understood and communicated quickly and clearly.

Although it's advisable to avoid repeating the same word, don't be too concerned about this. If you're writing about kitchen cutlery and you're selling self-sharpening knives, for instance, it's inevitable you're going to use the word *knife* often. Don't be tempted to call it a culinary implement or kitchen blade just to avoid repetition. It will cause the reader to pause and consider whether you're still referring to the knife, and you don't want your copy read in this halting way. **All copy needs to flow easily** whatever you're writing about.

Repeating a word can sometimes add emphasis to your message. In this instance you'll probably use the word three times in quick succession, such as: I'll guarantee the *best* accommodation, on the *best* island, at the *best* possible price!

To help the copy flow you need to **link each part of your copy effortlessly with the next.** You do this with the help of words and phrases such as:

- Here's how:

- Now we're set to change all that.

- I'm not stopping there . . .

- And that's not all.

- What's more . . .

- Sounds amazing?

By using these phrases you can make an easy transition from one subject to the next, as in:

. . . and we'll send you the matching linen pillowcase absolutely free. *But that's not all*, if your first order is over £50 we'll even . . .

Your writing should reflect how well you understand your reader, not your command of the language.

 MAKE IT PERSONAL

Wherever possible, make your writing personal. When you're writing sales letters, for instance, it's always preferable to write to a named individual. And computerisation has made personalisation much easier. You can now address your envelopes and letters to *Mr Michael Chequer* or *Mrs Rosemary Reynolds*, as appropriate. This immediately makes your letter more appealing than if you addressed it to: *Dear Householder* or *Dear Subscriber*.

Sometimes it isn't possible to address the letter personally so you have to choose an alternative, such as:

- Dear Customer
- Dear Reader
- Dear Dog Lover
- Dear Friend
- Dear Decorator.

The choice is yours, although **many copywriters prefer using *Dear Friend* if they can't use a personal salutation**.

Wherever possible too, it's good to **show the letter or statement coming from a named individual** – Christina Waugh, managing director, for instance, or David Price, chief buyer. This seems far more personal than Marketing Manager, ABC Limited. And the statement: *If you're not entirely satisfied, return to me, Kerry Dawn, at the following address* is more personal than *Return to Dept RG, if not satisfied*.

One important thing to remember about personalisation is that people get extremely disgruntled if you get something wrong. Take care not to write to Mr Kim Smith when you meant Mrs Kim Smith, or to spell their name Smith instead of Smythe. Many find it insulting too if you refer to them as a Marketing Assistant when they're the Marketing Director, or if you write to the Purchasing Manager when their correct title is Chief Buyer. So **check information** to ensure it's correct and up-to-date.

A clear, legible signature at the end of a sales letter works better than an illegible scrawl.

 WRITE ATTENTION-GRABBING HEADLINES AND SUBHEADINGS

Whatever you're writing you need to get people's attention. And **you do this by creating an attention-grabbing headline**. Because the headline is so important, spend at least half the time you've allowed for your whole project working on this alone. When you read or glance at a headline, you make a decision in seconds as to whether it's worth reading any further or not. Everyone does. And unless there's something in the headline which interests them, people won't read any further. Why should they? That's why **it's essential you put so much effort behind the headline**, as the rest of your copy won't even get read if the headline doesn't interest your reader.

Imagine you want to franchise your business. Your typical reader/buyer may be someone who is dissatisfied with working all hours, especially if they have little or no time or money left to get any enjoyment out of life. So, which of the following headlines do you think would bring the best response?

● *Franchise For Sale*

- *In One Year, I Cut My Working Time In Half And Doubled My Income*

The second one addresses your reader's problems. It offers a solution. It answers the 'what use is this to me?' question that anyone asks when they read a headline. And, everything else being equal, it will reap a better response. It also appears personal, from an individual, not an anonymous company or organisation. The headline also lets the reader know immediately what benefits are on offer. Many words and phrases have been proved to work well in headlines over and over again, including:

- How To . . .

- Secrets About . . .

- The Truth About . . .

- How I . . .

- Breakthrough . . .

- Discover . . .

- Do You . . .

Don't make the mistake of thinking your headline has to be clipped and short. Longer headlines using around 17 words often work better.

A good headline:

- Attracts the reader's attention.

- Expresses a major benefit.

- Appeals to the type of people you want to attract.

- Can be long.

Don't use misleading headlines. If you use a headline just to gain someone's attention and then talk about something completely different, you will irritate people and invariably they won't bother reading any further. If you write a headline which says: *I'm Offering Sex* it may grab your reader's attention. But when the copy goes on to say, *Right, now I've got your attention I'd like to tell you about my double-glazing company* . . . they'll feel cheated. And if you can cheat them over one thing, they'll believe you can cheat them over another.

Use lots of subheadings as they're useful to break up long tracts of text and make all copy easier to read. Some good examples are:

- Send No Money Now

- No Quibble Money Back Guarantee

- Easy To Use.

Well thought out subheadings act as signposts to the reader and will enhance your work greatly, provided they're followed by copy which is relevant.

Some copywriters spend as much as 80% of their allotted time working on the headline – that's how important the headline is.

 MAKE BODY COPY INTERESTING AND IMPORTANT
Many people assume that the shorter the body copy the better, but this isn't true. **Copy can never be too long, but it can be too boring.** In some instances you'll be restricted to the length of copy you can write because of the space available. If your words are to appear in a catalogue or on the reverse of a small display package, then your copy will need to be concise. But where you have more space, such as in a sales letter, your words need to flow freely, because if they're written too tightly they'll be a pain to read. When

writing sales letters you may do well to remember the saying **the more you tell the more you sell**. Look upon it as your opportunity to give the reader as much information as they need to come to a favourable decision about you, your product or service.

This isn't to say that you should waffle on at length about everything and anything. **Your body copy must be important, interesting and relevant if it's going to be read**. Sometimes you will have to include information which isn't necessarily interesting, but is important. If, after a page-and-a-half of copy, you feel you've written all you need, then stop. But if you need to write a six-page sales letter, take six pages, as long as you're sure you couldn't have expressed the same in less.

Always write with your reader in mind. Use words and phrases which are easily understood so they don't have to keep backtracking to grasp what you mean – they probably won't bother. Short words in short sentences are easy for everyone to read, but can be irritating if too clipped.

Make sure your body copy flows naturally by using snappy transitions, such as *after all* or *besides*. Every sentence and paragraph should flow effortlessly into the next. And put things in the right order. Don't put ordering information before you've explained exactly what it is you're offering. All copy needs to be organised so that it progresses in a logical sequence from the headline to the very last word. **Don't make information so difficult to find that people give up**. This is where subheadings are useful.

Be consistent in the way you write. If you start off in a relaxed, friendly style, don't suddenly switch to a formal, businesslike voice. Your reader will be aware of the change of tone and be confused by it. But if you send a package through the post which includes a sales letter and a brochure, you may consider varying the tone in those pieces. Write the letter in a friendly, positive, relaxed style, and the brochure in a tighter, more factual way.

Make all body copy as personal as you can. **Talk to the reader on a one-to-one basis**: use *I* and *me* and *you*. You're not a company offering a guarantee to some anonymous prospective purchaser, you're a person offering reassurance to a fellow man or woman. Everyone is important and your copy should reflect this.

Use dashes, or longer sentences followed by shorter ones. Anything that will add a sense of rhythm to your writing. Use bulleted lists. Not only do these visually break up the copy, they put key points into a memorable form. And if you use photographs within your copy, write a caption to accompany them.

Towards the end of your letter or advert, **you need to call your reader to action**. You've told them how your product will enhance their life, so now you must get them to act. Otherwise all your effort will have been wasted. Use phrases and words that urge them to respond in the way you want.

- Simply complete and return the enclosed order form today . . .

- Remember, this amazingly low price is valid for the next seven days only. So, don't delay.

- I invite you to call in and see for yourself . . .

- Send for our free full-colour catalogue.

- Ring me now on freephone . . . You'll be glad you did.

- Opportunity is just a phone call away. I'd like to hear from you.

If you don't tell the customer how to order the product, request a free trial or contact you, it's likely they won't. Ask for that order!

When writing a sales letter, always add a PS at the end. After the headline, this is the most read part of a letter and can double response. This is your last chance to emphasise your sales message. Use it to draw attention back to a major point you made in the body of your sales letter. Such as: *PS The 'Getting More Business' book has proved invaluable to small and medium sized companies every-where . . .*

Some people even put a PPS after a PS to reinforce or draw attention to another point. Look at your letter and use your discretion on this one.

You don't need to be miles better than your nearest competitor. Just one step ahead.

MAKING WHAT MATTERS WORK FOR YOU

✓ Become a wordsmith. Start looking and listening to words from a copywriter's viewpoint. Replace your old favourites with an alternative and gauge whether people react differently.

✓ Make a deliberate effort to express yourself in the easiest way possible – whether speaking or writing.

✓ Communicate with individuals – not businesses, charities or organisations.

✓ Command attention with your opening lines and present information in a logical sequence.

✓ Make all your words interesting and stimulating and ensure people know what action you want them to take.

3 Reassure the Reader

*The more you reassure your reader, the
more inclined they'll be to buy.*

5 things that really matter

1 **BE SPECIFIC**

2 **BE HONEST AND CREDIBLE**

3 **USE TESTIMONIALS AND REFERENCES**

4 **OFFER GUARANTEES**

5 **MAKE RESPONSE EASY**

The reader has read your copy and is seriously thinking of ordering your product. The size and colour are perfect and it has all the features they're looking for. It's not a bad price either, and it comes complete with bolt-on accessories (which are usually extra) and a chance to enter a free draw.

But the reader needs reassurance. Reassurance that what you're offering is exactly what it seems. That's because they've heard so many horror stories of how people have parted with money for things and then been let down. *'It didn't arrive when they said it would,'* is a common cry. And *'when it did it bore no resemblance to the way it was described in the advert.'* Maybe these things have happened to you. So you have the responsibility of writing **copy which will allay all their fears**.

IS THIS YOU?

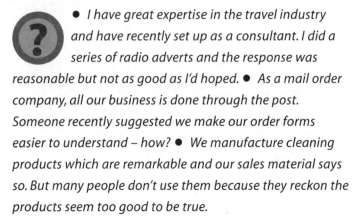

● *I have great expertise in the travel industry and have recently set up as a consultant. I did a series of radio adverts and the response was reasonable but not as good as I'd hoped.* ● *As a mail order company, all our business is done through the post. Someone recently suggested we make our order forms easier to understand – how?* ● *We manufacture cleaning products which are remarkable and our sales material says so. But many people don't use them because they reckon the products seem too good to be true.*

① BE SPECIFIC

How many times have you read advertisements, sales letters or other copy which talked about things being *great value*. Or perhaps they mentioned *experience* or *quality*. The trouble with words like *value*, *experience* and *quality* is that they're not necessarily positive qualities. Some people sell products and services which are *poor value* and of *inferior quality*. And the ten years experience they mention may have been *bad experience*. The problem is that words like these are so overused that people lose confidence in their meaning. So if you are going to use these words, ensure you **state exactly what you mean**.

Another area where it's essential to **be specific** is **when making comparisons**. You've probably seen slogans which read:

● lasts longer

● finishes the job faster

● works quicker

● moves better.

These are all hollow statements which will cause your reader to ask 'than what?' Your washing up liquid lasts longer than . . . ? Your service team finishes the job faster than . . . Your fertiliser works quicker than . . . ? And your van moves better than . . . ? If you are going to advertise in this way, be specific. Write in the answers to the questions. So if your stain remover works quicker than any other on the market, say so, and be specific.

Being specific is a very useful tool when writing copy for several reasons:

- The reader immediately knows what you're talking about.

- The reader doesn't make a wrong assumption.

- You don't have to write long descriptive passages.

Would you prefer to:

- Drink a beverage or an Irish coffee?

- Eat a dessert or a cream-topped chocolate mousse?

- Drive a car or a top-of-the-range Volvo estate?

Create an image for your reader that they can identify with. If you're talking about making money – say how much. If you're talking speed – say how fast. If the property you're selling is in a beautiful location – describe the location.

It's reassuring for people to have clear mental images.

 BE HONEST AND CREDIBLE

When writing your advertisement, sales letter, packaging or whatever sales message you're working on, make sure of your facts. Whatever claims you make – ensure you can substantiate them. If you can't, and someone picks you up on them, you'll be leaving yourself wide open to problems. If you're unsure about your product, service or any claims you make about it – resolve those issues first. **It's much easier to write about a product or service you have complete faith in than one you don't**. Above all, honesty pays because you're looking to build relationships, not to make a fast pound and disappear. You need to hang on to the people who buy from you. That's because **it's easier to sell something to someone who knows you, and what you are offering**. Repeat sales are great for business. So it makes sense to deliver all you claim in your copy.

Whatever you're selling you need to leave people with a favourable impression. That's why it makes sense to deliver exactly what you're offering – and a little bit more besides. That way people get more than they bargained for and you'll rise in their estimation.

Beware of knocking the competition as a way of promoting your own product. It can look as though you don't have enough to shout about regarding your own product so you're getting by through knocking someone else's. There's nothing to stop you showing a table, graph or similar graphic which clearly shows your product to be the fastest, cheapest or cleanest. It's better to concentrate on pushing your own product or service forward, however, rather than pulling others back.

Another thing that will raise your response rate is to offer your readers a free gift. It must be something that is worthwhile, a saleable item, such as a torch, mug, book or special report. There are obviously many more gifts you could offer and you need to assess which would work best with and enhance your products or services.

The next thing you need to consider is credibility. Because **your advertisement doesn't just have to be honest, it has to appear honest**, credible if you like. Otherwise people will think you're making exaggerated claims. If you read a headline which says *How 70 Year Olds Can Look Fifty Years Younger – in Minutes*, would you believe it? Chances are you wouldn't – even if it is true. So be careful not to make your product or service seem too good to be true or people will think it is.

Your advertisement doesn't just have to be honest, it has to appear credible too.

 USE TESTIMONIALS AND REFERENCES

The next time someone writes you a letter saying how pleased they are with your product or service – keep it. Ring the customer and ask if you can use their unsolicited testimonial in your future advertising. Usually, they're only too pleased. Or the next time someone rings and mentions how pleased they are with your service, ask them if they'd mind putting it in writing. Most people are happy to do so. Some people may say they're not much good at getting their thoughts and feelings down onto paper. In this instance, you could offer to write the letter for them. Then you send the letter to them for their approval and ask them to sign and return it. Make sure you write the testimonial using the sort of words and expressions your customer would use, however, otherwise it will appear false.

Using testimonials from satisfied customers is a great way to add extra leverage to your sales messages. After all, this isn't just you saying how good your products are, this is an unbiased third party saying how they have become more secure, intelligent, wealthy, confident or attractive by using what you're offering. They've tried the product, tested it, reaped the rewards and are now willing to shout about it!

A tip to remember when using testimonials is to use as full a name and address as possible. Consider the following:

> *C J says, 'I only ever use Stephen Wood's Antique Restoration Services. I recommend him time and time again.'*
>
> *Christopher James from Charmouth in Dorset says, 'I only ever use Stephen Wood's Antique Restoration Services. I recommend him time and time again.'*

Which testimonial would you find most believable? The last one, which uses a real name and place, sounds far more credible. How many of the *J B from England* and *T C from Hants* testimonials which appear daily in newspaper ads, magazines and sales letters do you find entirely convincing? Probably not many. They may well be true, but remember **they have to appear to be true** if you expect a customer to believe them.

Another place where an endorsement from a third party is good is in a lift letter or note. This is a letter or note which accompanies your main sales letter. Usually it's a smaller size, a single sheet folded in half. On the outside you write a few words which make the reader want to look inside – such as:

> *Read this only if you have decided not to order.*

And inside is a message from a third party which may start:

> *This risk-free offer is so good, I can't understand why everyone isn't clamouring to take advantage of it. I did, three years ago, and never looked back. My . . .*

Make sure this message is brief and genuine. Use paper that's different from your main letter and smaller (less than A4). It can even be handwritten.

The lift letter or note gives you another chance to persuade your reader to buy.

 OFFER GUARANTEES

To get the best response from your sales messages you need to **minimise risk** on behalf of your customer. Perhaps they won't respond to an ad because they're worried you will call at their home. So you write: *No salespeople will call*.

People are always concerned that they'll end up paying for something they don't want. Allay their fears by writing things such as:

- I'll post you this camera to examine FREE in the comfort of your own home.

- Send no money now.

- Test our camera for seven days – then decide!

- You never risk a penny.

Or, if they pay with the order:

- If you're not absolutely delighted, I'll buy it back – no questions asked.

Everyone likes guarantees. You like to know that if your new television is faulty, it will be exchanged without question; if your computer breaks down, it will be fixed promptly; and if the coat you bought through mail order doesn't fit, you can return it for a full refund.

Guarantee your customers that if a product or service doesn't live up to their expectations they won't be out of pocket. Offering guarantees often improves response. **Offering a money back guarantee always increases response**. So, if you're writing a sales letter, for instance, include phrases such as:

> *I personally guarantee that if you're not absolutely delighted your money will be promptly refunded – no questions asked.*

Or

> *I guarantee this organiser will bring order to your busy schedule. If, after examining its contents however, you're not 100% satisfied, please return it to me within 90 days for a full, no questions asked, refund.*

You may think that 90 days is too long a period for your customer to return your product – but this isn't so. The longer the guarantee period, the longer your customer has to test your products and services, and to discover how wonderful they are. It may also be that because they have such a long period, they forget to return them! Either way, **the longer the guarantee period you offer, the less returns you'll have**.

You don't have to offer just one guarantee. You can offer multiple guarantees, such as:

> *With Fletcher's Dental Plan I personally guarantee:*
> 1. *No rise in premiums for the next three years.*
> 2. *24 hour emergency service – 365 days a year.*
> 3. *If we keep you waiting more than 15 minutes for your appointment – we pay the next month's premium for you.*
>
> *That's my promise. And remember, you can cancel your premium at any time.*

You need to **constantly reassure the reader by offering guarantees**. Legally you're obliged to deliver what you offer anyway, so make a virtue of the fact.

Remember, never offer something you can't deliver.

MAKE RESPONSE EASY

Now that you have made your sales pitch, people have arrived at the moment of decision. **You need to keep on reassuring them**, urging them to go ahead and place that order. You can use many phrases to help your reader do this, including:

● Say Yes Now! Make this a turning point in your career.

● Don't hesitate and miss out on this . . .

● You won't find . . . in the shops, it's available only by mail order from . . .

● You have absolutely nothing to lose!

● Yes! I'm eager to know more about . . .

Above all you need to make it easy for your reader to respond. How do you want them to contact you – by post, telephone, fax, e-mail, through your web site or to call in person? Depending on which you choose, you can include statements such as:

● Call free on 0800 000 000.

● Fax us on 000 000 000 and we'll despatch your . . . within two days.

● Simply fill out the coupon below and post today.

● Choose one of the following for extra speedy delivery . . .

First **consider the outcome you want**. Do you want the reader to contact you for more details, or do you want them to buy direct from the page? Above all, if you're asking people to fill out an order or request form, make sure you've allowed sufficient space for them to do so. This is much easier when you're sending a sales letter as you can enclose a separate single sheet order form. Try printing the order form on a different colour paper from the rest of your sales material (letter, brochure, lift note) and, if you're offering a money back guarantee, why not head the form *Free Trial*. You are going to return their money anyway if they're not absolutely delighted, so make a selling point of it.

Above all, **the order form must be easy to understand and complete**. Consider printing the customer's name and address on order forms, or if you're labelling envelopes, attach a duplicate label to the form. This boosts response as they won't have to go through the bother of writing out all their contact details.

The less writing they have to do the better, so put tick boxes against statements, such as:

● Yes! Please rush me a copy of your book . . .

● I enclose a cheque for £7 (incl. p&p) made payable to . . .

● Please charge my Visa/Master card/Amex. (And put the correct number of spaces for their card number.)

Make life easy for them! Repeat your offer, main benefit, price, delivery details, and your customer's name and address on the order form. Write your contact name and number on there too, and tell them how to order and how to pay. **Treat the order form as a stand-alone device and ensure it has all the details on it they need**.

A freephone order line can increase your response as much as three times. Simply by changing three words from *call me now* to *call free now* can treble your response.

The order form is a vital part of your sales material – spend time making it look good and ensure it's easy to understand.

MAKING WHAT MATTERS WORK FOR YOU

✓ Mention things by name, be specific and avoid generalities.

✓ Be honest and avoid outrageous claims – remember you have to appear credible too.

✓ Use testimonials and endorsements to show how your product or service has benefited others.

✓ Offer a money back guarantee.

✓ Make it easy for readers to respond to what you're offering.

4 Avoid Copywriting Blunders

Always deliver more than you sell. Delivering more than you sell will leave the buyer with a good feeling, and they'll think favourably about you in the future.

5 things that really matter

1 **AVOID INDULGENT WRITING**

2 **AVOID CONFLICTING OR MISSING INFORMATION**

3 **AVOID LIFELESS WRITING**

4 **AVOID COMMON MISTAKES**

5 **STOP TRYING TO PLEASE EVERYBODY**

You don't want to waste a lot of time and money writing material which simply won't get read. You want to write great copy. **The fewer mistakes you make the better chance your words will have of making the right impact**. With hindsight, it's possible to see which things have worked consistently and reflect on what hasn't. There will always be exceptions because no two sets of circumstances are identical, and because times and attitudes change.

This chapter highlights those areas where you need to pay particular attention and looks at some of the most common copywriting mistakes. It answers the question, 'Can I please everybody?' and offers proven tips and techniques to greatly improve your chances of pulling together winning copy. But don't let the thought of making mistakes freeze you when writing. **It is much better to write regardless, than to write nothing for fear of not getting it exactly right**.

IS THIS YOU?

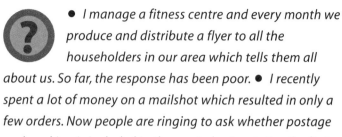

● I manage a fitness centre and every month we produce and distribute a flyer to all the householders in our area which tells them all about us. So far, the response has been poor. ● I recently spent a lot of money on a mailshot which resulted in only a few orders. Now people are ringing to ask whether postage and packing is included in the quoted price. ● For the first time I've been asked to write an advert for our limited edition plates. I'm so terrified of making an obvious error that I can't even get past the headline.

 ## AVOID INDULGENT WRITING

How many times have you read advertisements, sales letters or other copy which begins:

> *For 30 years we have worked from our fine Georgian premises providing quality accounting services to a wide range of clients . . .*

Now consider the following:

> *I reduced my tax bill by 50%, without earning a penny less. Here's how.*

You're far more likely to continue reading the second example because the introduction shows there is something in it for you. The first example is company-indulgent, and this is a common mistake people make when writing copy. They make the company appear more important than the reader. They assume the reader cares how long they've been in business, whether the company operates from fine old Georgian premises or a shop in the precinct. The reader doesn't.

All the material you write should be about what the company/product/person can do for the reader –

nothing else matters.

If you feel that the length of time you've been in business and other aspects of your company's background and production methods will interest your customers, you can put these details in a brochure. Or, if certain aspects are relevant in your sales material, put it at the stage where you're reassuring the reader – don't start your advert or letters with it.

If you've chosen to write copy, you probably love words. Because of this there is a real danger that your writing may become a little self-indulgent. This is a mistake. You must never let your literary skills get in the way of copy and its flow. **Your role is to write words which are readily understood and will persuade, reassure and motivate the reader to act in the way you desire**. This may be to sell a product, generate a sales lead, or raise public awareness of you, your company and its services.

Never let your literary skills get in the way of writing great copy.

 AVOID CONFLICTING OR MISSING INFORMATION

Be careful not to put **conflicting information** in your sales material. This may sound like common sense, but it is all too easy to do. Consider:

New and Improved Washup Liquid Soap

You see phrases like this – in adverts, on posters, in letters. But this is an example of conflicting information. How can something be improved if it's new? Something is either new or improved, it can't be both.

Thousands of people world-wide have photographic memories. And most have achieved this using Paul Aelsworth's Secret Memory Plan.

This is another example. Paul Aelsworth's Memory Plan isn't secret if thousands of people all over the world know about it.

Ensure too, that all the information you write is **consistent**. In your sales letter you may write:

> *I'll send you Gardener's Delight to try out FREE in the comfort of your own home for one month. Only then, when you are absolutely delighted, do you send any money . . .*

Imagine how confused the reader will be if you then write on the order form:

> *If you're not absolutely delighted with Gardener's Delight after 28 days, return to me and I'll give you a full refund.*

Another area where conflicting copy often occurs is **delivery**. If your copy reads *this time next week you could be sitting pretty on our . . .* and then elsewhere it reads *please allow 28 days for delivery . . .* The reader will be confused.

Check too that you haven't left out important information. What styles are available? What colours? What sizes? And have you included the products' order codes, technical specifications and the price? Does the price include VAT and delivery? If you are offering a series of goods, such as a set of limited edition plates or ceramics, ask yourself what you would want to know before committing yourself to buy. How many plates are there to collect in total? Do you receive a collector's certificate? Will the plate price remain the same throughout? Give the reader as much information as possible to help them reach a favourable conclusion about what you're offering. But always verify your facts. **Ensure you've left nothing vital out and check what you have said is consistent throughout.** If not, you'll confuse the reader and lose the sale. **See to it that the key**

facts are there for all to see. It's not up to your reader to hunt them out.

Remember, you can't offer a money back guarantee and then say, 'send no money now'.

 AVOID LIFELESS WRITING

Inject life into your writing. Don't write in a dull, monotone 'voice' as if every word is an effort to produce. Consider the following sentences:

You can become more assertive in under a month.

Be assertive in weeks!

The first is an example of passive writing, the second is active, direct and far more lively. The same applies to the following:

The room was improved by using the statue (passive).

The statue improves the room (active).

Use action words where possible – *tick, act, send, post, claim, choose, select, look*. And put people into your sentences. Don't talk about your production team, humanise them, give them names – Dylan Radcliffe and Emma Byron. And instead of simply listing a product's technical specifications, explain how those specs benefit the customer.

Don't use *etc*. Think of another way of rephrasing what you're saying. Instead of saying *our packs contain fresh peas, haricot beans, etc.* You could write *our packs contain many fresh vegetables including peas and haricot beans.* Or list a couple of items and end with . . . *and these are just a few.*

Short, three- or four-word sentences can add energy to your copy. *Call me now!* has more vitality than *If you feel* *you may be interested, then why not give me a call?* Too many short sentences can cause your copy to be stilted and difficult to read, however, so use these with care.

An ellipsis (three full stops . . .) can add pace to weary copy too. *Call me now . . . You'll be glad you did.* But too many of these will be irritating to read so, use with care.

If you're saying something's scented, think of colourful words to express it – *intoxicating, fragrant, aromatic, bracing, delicate, perfumed* as in *. . . aromatic Spanish cedar lines this exquisite box.*

Above all, don't write lifeless passive copy which sounds as if you have no enthusiasm for the product, the day or the job. If this is the case, and you really can't get enthused, put the copy to one side until you can. Otherwise you will write indifferent words, and it will show. Better then to make sure you're in the right frame of mind before you start. Whenever possible:

- Use a quick relaxation technique to rid your mind and body of tension.

- Visualise yourself writing great copy by a set time limit.

- Use positive affirmations to get yourself into an enthusiastic frame of mind – *I love my job and all that I do.*

- Don't overeat before sitting down to write.

- Don't allow interruptions.

Approaching your copywriting in a good frame of mind works wonders for your copy. If you're feeling tired, rundown or fed up, work on changing the way you feel – and watch your writing improve dramatically.

Don't write in a dull, monotone 'voice' as if every word is an effort to produce.

AVOID COMMON MISTAKES

There are some mistakes which crop up in advertising, promotional and packaging copy time after time. Many examples have already appeared in this book and more follow.

- **Needlessly complex phrases and words**. *When you come into contact with the manager . . .* could be simplified to *when you meet the manager.* Rather than write *He was promoted by virtue of the fact that . . .* simplify it to *He was promoted because . . .* and it's the same with words. Don't write *methodology* when you mean *method.* Clarity is essential.

- **Misuse of You're and Your**. Make sure you understand when to use *you're* and when to use *your.* The apostrophe (') in *you're* indicates that the letter *a* is missing, as the word is a contraction of you are. *You're about to be amazed* is an example of this. Whereas *your* indicates possession, such as *your career, your Mercedes* or *your holiday.*

- **No call to action**. At the end of your advertisement, letter, copy, you almost always need to get the reader to do something. Send a coupon, order or telephone. Make sure the reader knows what's expected of them and you'll turn a prospect into a customer.

- **Overlong sentences**. Sentence length should vary naturally as you write. Some will be short and punchy. Others will be longer, between eight to 15 words perhaps. Sentences longer than this could be rewritten as two sentences.

- **Misuse of quotation marks**. You can use quotation

marks to indicate a word or saying isn't meant to be taken literally. Consider: *The 'famous' guest came to stay.* The use of quotation marks around the word famous indicates the guest wasn't famous at all, the reverse in fact. But some copywriters mistakenly put quotation marks around words which are meant to mean exactly what they say. If you put quotation marks around *'antiques'*, you're implying they're not antiques. In the same way, if you refer to *'fresh' meat*, you're suggesting the meat isn't fresh.

- **Copy is upside down**. Remember to start all your copy by showing how your product or service benefits the reader. Don't write your material upside down by starting off with information about you and your company and end by telling them how your products and services benefit them. You'll lose the reader in seconds.

- **Misuse of it's and its**. The apostrophe (') in *it's* shows a letter is missing as the word is a contraction of the two words *it is*. *It is too good an offer to miss* can also be written *It's too good an offer to miss*. *Its* however indicates possession, and as a possessive pronoun it never has an apostrophe. *The director's car flashes its hazard warning lamps* and *The offer had lost its appeal* are examples of this.

- **Messages with double meanings**. *At the age of 17, her mother died.* This sounds as if the mother was 17 when she died. But if you rewrite it: *At the age of 17, Molly lost her mother* it becomes clear that it was Molly who was 17 when her mother died. Look at the following two sentences:

I almost lost all of my money.
I lost almost all of my money.

Both are grammatically correct, but you'll notice they convey different meanings.

- **Don't write misleading headlines.** Don't use curiosity or misleading headlines just to get your readers' attention. They won't be able to fully trust you from then on.

- **Don't misuse humour.** What one person might find funny, another will find shallow. What might cause one person to laugh out loud will cause another to gasp in horror. Reaction to humour is personal. Because of this it is best to leave humour out of your copy. Your copy needs to be friendly, but avoid puns and elbow-in-the-ribs type jokes unless you're entirely sure of your audience.

Next time you pass an advertisement by without a second look, return to it and ask yourself why.

 STOP TRYING TO PLEASE EVERYBODY

It's a mistake to try to please everybody, because you never will. Before setting out to write you need to consider who your typical reader will be – and then write to that one person.

If you're writing copy to promote your own product or service then you have no one to answer to but yourself. **If your copy is brilliant, results will prove this in the same way they will if your copy is terrible.** You will have a free hand to experiment with different copy in different publications. The challenge with writing your own copy is to remain objective. You know everything there is to know about your product or service, and you may forget your reader doesn't. So if you come up with a point and then change your mind, thinking everybody knows about it, remember that they probably don't.

If you're copywriting for a company department or organisation, it's likely you'll have to please many more people. And people can't resist making changes to other people's copy – even if it's just a word. But as a copywriter you know the difference a word can make. So, if you're really unhappy with someone's request for changes, say so. But do **listen and reflect on other people's comments**. They are looking at your words with a fresh eye and can sometimes point out something you've missed or suggest where something needs expanding.

Copywriters know all about good grammar, although their copy isn't always grammatically correct. Their challenge is to **use and structure words in a way that will elicit a particular response** from the reader. So if your grammar is called into question, check it. And if you feel the grammatical changes will improve your copy, implement them.

The one person you should concentrate on pleasing is the reader.

MAKING WHAT MATTERS WORK FOR YOU

✓ Avoid talking about yourself and your company – especially initially. Turn everything around to how it can benefit the reader.

✓ Make sure you don't give conflicting messages or wrong information. And if you want the reader to do something – tell them what and give them the necessary information.

✓ Write in a lively, active style, not in a passive fashion.

✓ Familiarise yourself with common copywriting mistakes – and avoid them!

✓ Never try to please everyone – it's impossible. Try to please one person when you write – the reader, the prospect, your target.

5 How to Improve All Copy

Improve your copy, make it excellent,
but remember too that perfection can equal paralysis.

5
things that
really matter

1 **REFRAME WHAT'S ON OFFER**

2 **CONSIDER STYLE, SIZE AND LAYOUT**

3 **USE PROVEN TECHNIQUES**

4 **EDIT RUTHLESSLY**

5 **TEST AND REVIEW**

Congratulations! You've finished writing your copy. Are you happy with it? Do you read it and think, 'Did I write this wonderful advertisement, sales letter or commercial?' Or do you realise it needs improving but don't know where to start? Whatever your particular challenge, this section of the book has something for you, because **all copy can be improved**.

Perhaps you can rephrase what you're offering to make it sound more inviting, more tempting. And if you're responsible for the overall look of your words when they appear in print, there's help with that too, with tips on **choosing a typeface** and techniques to ensure **maximum readability**. Then it's on to **editing and revising** and that final tweak to ensure your work isn't just good – it's great! And, just when you thought you were finished, it's on to **testing**. With so much money riding on every word, you can't possibly leave anything to guesswork.

IS THIS YOU?

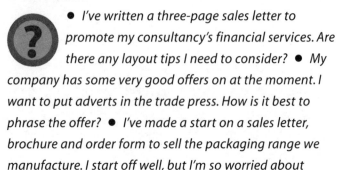

● *I've written a three-page sales letter to promote my consultancy's financial services. Are there any layout tips I need to consider?* ● *My company has some very good offers on at the moment. I want to put adverts in the trade press. How is it best to phrase the offer?* ● *I've made a start on a sales letter, brochure and order form to sell the packaging range we manufacture. I start off well, but I'm so worried about getting it wrong that I never get further than a couple of paragraphs on each.*

 REFRAME WHAT'S ON OFFER

Simply rephrasing what you're offering can make a tremendous difference to the response you get. As a general rule, try to write in a positive rather than negative form. This often involves replacing the word *not*, as shown here:

> *We're not about to go out of business*

becomes

> *We're here to stay!*

> *We will not let you down*

becomes

> *You can always count on us.*

You need to use your discretion regarding negative statements, as sometimes you can work them to your advantage – test and see.

Another way to rephrase is to give your reader the problem first, then offer the solution. So, instead of talking about a wonderful new car upholstery cleaner, you might say:

> *Are you ashamed of the upholstery in your car?*

And then lead into the solution – your effective fabric cleaner.

Perhaps you have a special offer on your product or service and have slashed your prices by 50%. Instead of writing *prices slashed by 50%*, consider putting *two for the price of one*, or even better *buy one get one free!* Instead of saying *25% off your annual premium*, consider *3 months rental absolutely free!* Offer incentives too. Say that if the reader replies by a given date, you'll give them an extra month free, or two free months the following year (this ties them into you for two years). *Order within ten days and I'll insure your dog free for the first three months.* Or offer a year's free subscription to a topic related magazine, one that you know would really interest the reader: *And if you order within seven days, you'll receive a year's free subscription to Dog Lovers magazine.*

Encourage future sales too: *build up a valuable collection of limited edition signed prints by the well-loved artist* . . .

Above all, **constantly remind yourself of who you're writing to**. What would you want if you were them? Answer that question and reframe your offer to fit.

 CONSIDER STYLE, SIZE AND LAYOUT

Whatever you're writing, it will have to appear either in print (such as in newspaper and magazine ads, direct mail, posters, or on packaging) or as the spoken word (radio, video and TV commercials). You will have established this before you write as you obviously need to know how much space you have to play with. **In addition to what you say, the way your words look is another factor in determining whether all your hard work is even read or not**. You may not have control over the way the final piece is put together, but if you are responsible or do have a say, the following additional tips will help.

Sales letters

- If you are writing a sales letter, are you simply writing it on your usual headed paper? It would be much better if you used the space at the top of the page for your attention-grabbing headline. You can put all your contact details and logo at the end of the letter on the final page.

- Don't use justified text where the lines of text are perfectly equal in length the whole way through as this can be difficult to read. A left-aligned (ragged right) margin (like this) is far easier to read.

- For maximum legibility, a line length of around 60 characters is preferable.

- Make sure the typeface you've chosen is easy to read and suits the product or service you're selling. A flowery script, for instance, can be difficult to read. It would be inappropriate too if you're selling a high-tech product.

- Break up the copy with lots of subheadings and paragraphs.

Packaging copy

Ensure your copy includes what you legally need to show. This may be a list of ingredients, contents, warnings, or a notice stating that the product or service conforms with legal requirements. Perhaps you want to alert customers to the fact that your product may contain traces of nuts, that genetically modified soya has not been used, or that it contains small parts unsuitable for children under 3 years of age. Packaging copy doesn't have to be a bland list of facts, however. **Use it in the same way you would any other sales opportunity**. If it's new, improved, quick to prepare, or comes with a free spoon, pen or diary – say so! If it's a hobby style product, say that easy-to-read instructions are inside. Or if the instructions are on the packaging, ensure they are easy to understand. **Pay as much attention to writing excellent packaging copy as you would to any other sales message**. It doesn't matter how great the product is inside, if the packaging doesn't grab attention or inspire confidence in the buyer, it won't sell.

Adverts

The points regarding typeface and font style mentioned under sales letters are equally relevant here. Also, if you're including a clip-out order form on the advertisement, ensure there's adequate space for the reader to fill out the relevant details, or offer a telephone order line.

Using a photograph in an advertisement often increases response. Generally, pictures of humans are better than pictures of products. You can, of course, have both in the same shot. Whichever you use, ensure there is a clear link between the photo and the product. And write a caption.

Commercials, TV, radio, videos

Whatever you decide to write remember where it will be heard and/or seen. On the radio you won't be able to accompany it with strong images so you will need to be particularly clear about what you're offering and how and where the listener can get it. **Keep it as simple as you can and talk to the listener direct on a one-to-one basis**.

TV commercials and video presentations are frequently

enjoyed but afterwards people often can't remember the product or service that was being advertised! Be creative by all means, but **above all be effective**.

 ### USE PROVEN TECHNIQUES

Every copywriter has their own ideas about what works for them. A large part of it is based on instinct, which is later borne out by results. But **given the benefit of time, it's possible to see what has consistently increased a copy's effectiveness**. As with every skill, the results often depend on a large number of factors. You may have written the best newspaper ad of all time, but if there's a spate of random strikes that day and distribution is limited, you'd obviously be unwise to base the inevitably poor results on that one trial. But, all things being equal, and in addition to all you've already read, here are just some of the elements that appear to consistently improve readability and response.

- Use a serif typeface for text, especially body text. This is a serif typeface. This is a sans serif typeface. Notice how the strokes of the serif typeface have 'tails' on them – the T for example has two at its base and one at each end of the top cross bar. This makes it easier to read, especially in large tracts of text.

- The size of the typeface is important too. Eleven is a good size for a sales letter written in a Times New Roman or Palatino style, for example. On a poster it would be far too small. Use your judgement, but remember, too big can look too gawky, almost amateurish. Too small and your reader won't bother to strain their eyes.

- Sign a sales letter in blue ink (not black). And if you're printing 'handwritten' margin notes, put these in blue too. Reflex blue is considered the best to use.

- Print your order form on one side only, and print it on a different type of paper than the rest of your mailing.

- Offer a money back guarantee.

- Always put a caption with a photo.

- Include a brochure in a direct mail package.

- Brochures should include features and benefits and repeat the offer.

- Finish sentences in mid-air at the bottom of a sales letter so the reader has to turn to the next page to complete it.

- Don't use too much (if any) reverse print – white on black – it's not easy to read.

- Sales letters can be too long and they can be too short. Let the copy flow effortlessly to reach its natural conclusion.

- Use testimonials.

- Don't stop the reader in mid flow. If you write . . . *and this timesaving device (as shown overleaf)* . . . the reader *will* turn over and miss the carefully constructed flow of the sales copy that you've worked so hard on.

- Don't forget to close the sale with a persuasive call to action – *Yes! Please rush me the . . . Send no money today. I'm happy to invoice you after you've had an opportunity to try this revolutionary dirt-buster in the privacy of your home.* You must ask for the order or you will lose the sale.

 EDIT RUTHLESSLY

Now that you've finished writing the copy, you move on to the editing process. If you have time to set it aside, untouched for a day or two, do so. If, like many copywriters, you are working to tight deadlines and don't have time to do this, **set it aside for a while anyway** – even if it's only for 15 minutes. Go for a drink, to the toilet, walk around the office or, even better, outside in the fresh air – anywhere away from your copy. And if you're thinking, 'I simply don't have time to do this,' *do it anyway*. It will pay great dividends as you will return more objective, more decisive and with clearer thinking.

Use the copywriter's checklist at the end of this chapter to make sure you've included all you need. Check your facts to make sure you've got them correct, including product sizes, colours, codes, claims. If you've said postage and packing is extra, have you said how much? Have you said how long before the item is despatched? Have you covered your legal requirements? If you've included boxes for readers to put their credit card numbers in, have you put enough boxes? Ensure you haven't left anything out.

If you have someone who can read it to you, ask them to do so once – from start to finish without stopping. **Listen carefully to the flow of your copy with someone else reading it**. Do they put the same emphasis where you do? If not, will your reader? Is it clear and easy to read? Does it grab or excite you? Do you want to buy, respond, or do you think, 'Um, that's OK' and go right back to what you were doing before?

Now read it aloud to yourself, cutting out every unnecessary word, whilst ensuring it still flows and check spelling, punctuation and grammar.

If you're not happy with what you've written, go back over the steps in this book and produce another draft. But don't make changes for the sake of it, and don't throw away your first drafts. You might well return to your first ideas and realise they were the best.

The opinion of others is useful but if they're not copywriters you can't expect them to understand the reasoning behind the way you've done things. If an illustrator asks someone about his work, they invariably say, 'That's great,' and leave it at that because they can't draw. But show someone your copy and they're likely to grab a pen and start adding and deleting words, rearranging phrases, and generally offering 'useful' advice because, of course, they can write!

Whatever you're editing, there comes a stage where you must make a decision and stick to it. **Give yourself a deadline if one isn't enforced upon you and stick to it**. Be your own critic.

 TEST AND REVIEW

It's imperative that you test the effectiveness of your copy by monitoring response. If you put an advertisement in the newspaper, for example, but don't ask customers how they came to know about you, you'll never know if a hundred people bought from you as a result of that advertisement or just one. It's important to have systems in place that allow you to test the response you get.

A useful form of testing is to try out two different options at the same time. But vary only one element at a time, of course, such as the headline, otherwise you won't know which variable caused the difference. Remember too that testing needs to be an ongoing process as the marketplace is constantly changing. But if something is working well – leave it. Certainly don't make changes just for the sake of it.

Test different elements of your copy and design in addition to timing, target audience, pricing, discounts, incentives, product specifications or service terms – anything which might make a difference.

If you've sent out a mailshot with a variable, you need to put some sort of reference number or code on the order or response cards so you can see which worked best. Or if you've put a telephone contact number on, staff taking the calls need to ask for the reference number. **Test on a regular basis to discover which element of your copy works best, and which ones don't work at all**.

The Royal Mail says that in mailshots the response level most businesses expect is between 1% and 5%. These figures do vary, of course, from mailing to mailing and industry to industry, and the people you mail to (the mailing list) can produce significant changes to response.

You need to test big differences, such as testing an advertisement with and without a free offer, or a mailshot with or without a 50% discount. Don't make small changes, such as offering one with a 15% discount and one with a 12% discount as it's not a significant difference.

Above all, you need to see what works for you. Input from other companies, individuals, copywriters, markateers is valuable, but everyone's set of circumstances is different, even if only slightly. Test, and see what works for you.

COPYWRITER'S CHECKLIST

When your copy is complete, check that you can say 'Yes' to the following:

- Copy is written to a specific reader.

- The headline grabs attention.

- The benefits are clear.

- Copy is persuasive and interesting.
- Copy holds reader's attention throughout.
- Facts are correct.
- Copy is free of spelling and punctuation errors.
- Copy flows easily.
- The style and language used are appropriate.
- The style and language used are consistent.
- Contact details are clear.
- Instructions are clear.
- Copy includes a call to action.
- Reader knows how to respond.
- There is no missing or conflicting information.
- I'm happy with this copy.

MAKING WHAT MATTERS WORK FOR YOU

✓ Identify different ways of offering your product or service.

✓ Use the most appropriate typeface to ensure your words look as great as they sound, and consider layout and type size too.

✓ Become familiar with the techniques professional copywriters use, and incorporate them into your copy.

✓ Learn how to remain objective throughout the editing process and be your own critic.

✓ Test, review, appraise, compare, anything that ensures you are getting the results you deserve.